TRUST

STUDY GUIDE

TRUST

STUDY GUIDE

KNOWING WHEN TO GIVE IT,
WHEN TO WITHHOLD IT,
HOW TO EARN IT, AND HOW TO
FIX IT WHEN IT GETS BROKEN

HENRY CLOUD

NASHVILLE   NEW YORK

Worthy
Hachette Book Group
1290 Avenue of the Americas, New York, NY 10104
worthypublishing.com
twitter.com/worthypub

First Edition: March 2023

Worthy is a division of Hachette Book Group, Inc. The Worthy name and logo
are trademarks of Hachette Book Group, Inc.

The publisher is not responsible for websites (or their content) that are not
owned by the publisher.

Worthy Books may be purchased in bulk for business, educational, or
promotional use. For information, please contact your local bookseller or the
Hachette Book Group Special Markets Department at special.markets@
hbgusa.com.

ISBN: 9781546003380 (trade paperback)

Printed in the United States of America

LSC-C

Printing 2, 2023

CONTENTS

TRUST

STUDY GUIDE

Do not forsake wisdom, and she will protect you; love her,
and she will watch over you.

— Proverbs 4:6 NIV

INTRODUCTION

Hello, and welcome to this study guide for *Trust*.

As you will see throughout these pages, trust is a foundational element for just about every aspect of human life. It is essential for happiness, success, and fulfillment. For these reasons and more, I am grateful you have chosen to trust me as your guide through this critical topic, and I am excited for everything you will experience throughout this resource.

We're going to cover a lot of ground in these pages. We'll examine what trust is, why it is necessary, how to build it, how to repair it, and how to avoid making the same mistakes that keep causing damage in our lives.

My goal is for you to become an expert in your own unique needs and abilities connected to this critical proficiency we call trust.

As you work through the material, you'll notice that each of the eight sessions is divided into two sections: one for personal study, and the other for group discussion. That first element is necessary because growth and development can be boosted by comprehension. Learning helpful information and skills allows us to change not just what we do, but *why* we do it.

Yet the second element—group discussion—is also critical. Learning something new is only half the battle. It is crucial to apply that knowledge in real-world situations in order to truly incorporate the new information into your actions and attitudes. And that kind of practice is greatly enhanced when you have the help and support of others.

Before we get started with session 1, let me say that my goal for you in engaging this study guide is more than informational—it's transformational. I want these pages to change your life for the better.

When combined with the *Trust* book, the content in this study guide can be a catalyst for that kind of change. Therefore, I hope you'll do the work of engaging these pages with honesty and sincerity.

If so, I'm confident you will be rewarded.

—Dr. Henry Cloud

THE NECESSITY OF TRUST

In this session, you will:

- Learn what trust is and why it is necessary in our lives.
- Explore the reality that human beings are wired for trust at our most basic levels.
- Review a brief overview of the five essentials of trust.
- Join with others to review these themes and discuss how they apply to your lives and your community.

> Prior to engaging this session, read chapters 1–3 in the *Trust* trade book.

Personal Study

There are many concepts in our culture that are simultaneously known and unknown. They are easy to understand in a general sense yet difficult to define in any specific way.

Take peace, for example. If I said to you, "Be at peace," or, "You need to build more peace in your life," you would understand what I'm saying. On a general level, you and I both know what we mean by the word *peace*.

But if I asked you to write out a definition of peace, or if I asked you to draw a picture of what peace looks like in your daily routine, that would take some deeper thinking. How does peace become manifested in your specific life as a unique individual? Is it the absence of conflict? The absence of pain? Is it the presence of healthy relationships? Is it having enough time to achieve your goals each day? Is it the luxury of an afternoon nap?

The same principle applies to most high-level concepts that impact us as individuals. Happiness. Wealth. Fear. Faith. Depression. Love.

And trust.

As I wrote on p. 4 of the *Trust* trade book: "Trust is the fuel for all of life. Nothing in life works without it—especially relationships. We are wired biologically, neurologically, emotionally, spiritually, and psychologically to trust. Trust is the currency that drives everything."

As one of the foundations of human society, trust is too important to leave in the realm of generalities. We must not settle for vagueness when contemplating what it means to trust other people and what it means to live as a person who can be trusted. For that reason, let's begin this session by getting more specific.

How would you define the concept of "trust" in your own words? What is it?

_____

_____

_____

_____

Use the space below to list three people whom you actively trust. Next to each name, write a brief explanation of why you trust that person.

1. _____

2. _____

3. _____

"Trust no one" has been a popular motto for decades. Many people believe that they live outside of the need for trust. They carefully cultivate a guarded stance in their relationships with family, friends, coworkers, organizations, and even God out of a desire to protect themselves from being required to trust.

Such people are fooling themselves. Trust is a necessity for all people in every phase of our lives.

Consider this excerpt from page 22 of the *Trust* trade book:

> Think about this: As human beings, our natural chemical makeup is designed to trust and to bond. We literally can't help it. God wired us this way, as Scripture attests, as a beautiful first step in even trusting Him: "You made me trust in you, even at my mother's breast" (Ps. 22:9 NIV).
>
> Humans are literally wired for trust, as trust is the fuel and currency that makes all of life work, from the very beginning until the very end. Placing our trust in other human beings makes every system develop. This happens emotionally, as a child grows and develops. It happens physically, as the emotional attachment that trust brings causes brains to develop normally, immune systems to function, body weight to hit normal levels, brain sizes to achieve milestones, and on and on. It takes place socially, as the child enlarges his or her circle of trust to include more than parents and family members and ultimately includes friends and peers. Trust begets more trust. And this happens professionally, as he or she enters the world of commerce, which can only function if trust is secure. For example, if we cannot trust our markets, the entire financial system comes tumbling down, as we see when trust is leaky, such as in 2008.
>
> Trust is the most important tool we have in life, in every area. Nothing works without it.
>
> The argument I am making here is crucial for our understanding of trust: It is *not* optional if we are going to have a good life or realize any kind of success. Period.

Where do you see evidence in your community that trust is a necessary part
of human life?

_____

_____

_____

_____

What are some of the main ways you have benefited from trusting others
in recent years?

_____

_____

_____

_____

When have you suffered harm because you trusted a person or an organization
that was not worthy of that trust?

_____

_____

_____

_____

It's common for people to perceive trust only as an emotional response. A feeling. Something we experience in our gut rather than our brain. There is some truth
to that approach. There are times when we can have an intuitive reaction to people,
organizations, or situations that give us strong guidance for the best way to respond.

There are individuals who have the ability to discern and assess trustworthiness in a way that is almost instinctual.

But that is not the most complete way for us to approach questions of trust. Feelings can be fooled. What seems like a positive connection can quickly turn into a nightmare relationship. How often we feel the sting of these painful words: "I thought I could trust . . ."

We are better served to approach issues of trust not only as moments for interpreting feelings but as opportunities to make decisions based also on data. The question "Can I trust you?" is answerable. It's definable because trust is definable.

Specifically, trust is rooted in these five essential qualities:

1. **Understanding**: Does the person (or organization) in question understand who you are and what you need?
2. **Motive**: The "Why?" question. What motivations are driving a potential interaction or relationship?
3. **Ability**: Is the person (or organization) in question truly able to provide what you need? Can they be trusted in the specific ways that you need to depend on them in the situation or circumstance that has brought you together?
4. **Character**: This essential speaks to how the person (or organization) is wired on the deepest levels. Do they possess the moral qualities necessary for trust? Do they possess the other personal qualities that you will need from them besides "moral" integrity?
5. **Track Record**: The best predictor of the future is the past. So, what does this person's (or organization's) past say about their trustworthiness in the present?

Review the story of Shannon and Colin from pp. 27–38 of the *Trust* book. In that story, Shannon and Colin engage five questions designed to help them evaluate a relationship based on the five essentials of trust listed above.

Let's conduct an exercise to help ground these five essentials in real-life circumstances. To begin, think of a company, an organization, or a person with whom (or which) you currently feel conflict or tension. Use the space below to describe what makes you feel dissatisfied about your interactions with that company, organization, or person.

Next, work through the following questions to evaluate your relationship with them based on the five essentials of trust. Each question includes a scale of 1 to 5, with 1 being the lowest score.

1. To what degree does the company, organization, or person understand what you are looking to receive from your relationship? How well do they understand your needs?

      1   2   3   4   5

2. How much do you feel their motives are based on satisfying you rather than meeting their own needs?

      1   2   3   4   5

3. To what degree are they capable of meeting your needs? Do they have the capacity to satisfy you?

      1   2   3   4   5

4. How pleased do you feel about the character or integrity of the company, organization, or person?

      1   2   3   4   5

5. Given their track record in the past—their performance for both you and others—how confident do you feel they can meet your needs in the future?

      1   2   3   4   5

Based on your answers above, which of the five essentials of trust have been deficient in your reliance upon the company, organization, or person in question?

_____

_____

_____

_____

It's time to look at the other side of the mirror. The issues impacting and affecting trust in our lives run both ways. Meaning, it's useful and helpful to assess our interactions with other people and organizations based on the five essentials of trust—and that is what we'll be doing over the next two sessions in this study guide. But it's also critical for us to evaluate ourselves based on those essentials.

In other words, are you and I worthy of trust? Of being trusted? In what areas do we need to grow in order to repay the trust that others have invested in us?

Here is another way of phrasing the five essentials of trust:

1. People can trust you when they feel you deeply understand, feel, and care about their needs.
2. People can trust you when they feel your motive is "for" them, not just for yourself.
3. People can trust you when they believe you have the ability to meet their needs and deliver results.
4. People can trust you when they feel confident in your personal character and internal makeup.
5. People can trust you when you demonstrate a track record of performing in the ways they need you to perform.

Based on those five essentials, where do you see evidence in your life that
suggests you are a person who should be trusted?

_____

_____

_____

_____

In which of the five essentials do you have the most room for growth?
What makes you choose that one?

_____

_____

_____

_____

GROUP DISCUSSION

Icebreaker

Choose one of the following questions to begin your group's discussion on "The Necessity of Trust."

- What are the primary images that come to your mind when you hear the word "trust"? Why?

  or

- When has a corporate brand done something to earn your trust in a big way?

Content Review

What ideas or principles did you find most interesting from chapters 1–3 of *Trust*?

_____

_____

_____

_____

What questions have been on your mind since reading those chapters? Or, what seemed confusing that you'd like to have resolved?

_____

_____

_____

_____

Look again at this paragraph from p. 12 of *Trust*:

> You know your history of broken trust. You know who was involved,
> and you know what happened. The list of ways humans can betray
> one another is almost infinite, but the pain is always the same: hurt,
> betrayal, disillusionment, anger, withdrawal from trusting others,
> reticence in future transactions, suspicion, and more. In short, when
> trust is broken and we are betrayed, we suffer.

What does it mean for trust to be "broken"? Work as a group to set some specific parameters or definitions around that phenomenon.

_____

_____

_____

How have betrayals and broken trust influenced the person you are today?

_____

_____

_____

Chapter 2 makes the case that human beings are wired for trust. Given that reality, what are some possible reasons why trust is so difficult to achieve and maintain?

_____

_____

_____

Look again at the five essentials of trust:

1. **Understanding**
2. **Motive**
3. **Ability**
4. **Character**
5. **Track Record**

Which of those essentials feels most lacking in our culture?

_____

_____

_____

Which of these essentials have you found to be the biggest challenge when considering whether or not someone is trustworthy? Why?

_____

_____

_____

Case Study

Sarah is preparing for a meeting with her daughter's high school principal. There have been recurring instances of bullying in recent weeks involving Sarah's daughter Rachel.

According to Rachel, several students in her class have been teasing her and ridiculing her because of a photo she posted on social media. Rachel erased the photo after the first incident, but other students had already saved it. Every few days, those students find a way to tease or embarrass Rachel with that picture.

Sarah has already had several conversations with various teachers at the school, and they all seem convinced that the incident has been resolved. The aggressors were told to delete the photo and to stop their behavior. But Rachel says they are teasing her now in ways that cannot be traced or confirmed.

As a working mom, Sarah is already feeling exasperated in advance of this meeting with the principal. She needs this situation to be resolved.

Where do you see specific opportunities for the principal (and/or the school) to earn Sarah's trust in this scenario?

_____

_____

_____

_____

Work as a group to review Sarah's situation in light of the five essentials of trust.

- **Understanding**: What does Sarah want the school to understand about her needs? Her daughter's needs?
- **Motive**: Where do you see a possible clash between the school's motives and Sarah's needs?
- **Ability**: Think through all the people involved in this scenario—Sarah, Rachel, the bullies, the teachers, and the principal. Who might have the ability to resolve things successfully?
- **Character**: What virtues or character traits are needed to achieve a successful resolution?
- **Track Record**: What steps can Sarah take to assess the school's track record on the issue of bullying?

Wrap Up

Remember these truths as you conclude this discussion of session 1:

- Trust is a critical foundation not only of our culture at large but of the specific relationships and interactions that make up your everyday life.
- All people are hardwired for trust.
- The decision to trust a person or an organization is just that—a decision. It's a choice we can make based on evidence and logic, as well as instinct and emotion.

What is one action you would like to take this week based on what you've learned?

_____

_____

_____

_____

Blessed is the man who trusts in the Lord,

And whose hope is the Lord.

For he shall be like a tree planted by the waters,

Which spreads out its roots by the river,

And will not fear when heat comes;

But its leaf will be green,

And will not be anxious in the year of drought,

Nor will cease from yielding fruit.

— Jeremiah 17:7–8 NKJV

THE ESSENTIALS OF TRUST (PART 1)

In this session, you will:

- Dig deeper into the first essential of trust: understanding.
- Dig deeper into the second essential of trust: motive.
- Seek to engage those essentials by exploring real-world examples and circumstances.
- Join with others to review these themes and discuss how they apply to your lives and your community.

Prior to engaging this session, read chapters 4–5 in the *Trust* trade book.

Personal Study

Just about everyone enjoys great food. But people don't always understand that great meals require great ingredients.

Someone launching a new restaurant could hire the very best chef and a top-notch staff. They could invest in state-of-the-art equipment and display a professionally polished décor. They could even bring in live music for the perfect atmosphere. But if that restaurant relies on frozen, prepackaged ingredients from the back of a truck, the meals served there will be virtually indistinguishable from those served at the eateries found alongside highway exits.

There is a similar dynamic at play when it comes to trust. Everyone wants to experience trust, both giving and receiving. But when we don't understand the essential ingredients that produce trust, the outcome is mediocre at best. And that leaves us with a bad taste in our mouth.

As a reminder, these are the five essential elements that produce trust in today's world:

1. **Understanding**: Does the person or organization in question understand who you are and what you need?
2. **Motive**: The "Why?" question. What motivations are driving a potential interaction or relationship?
3. **Ability**: Is the person or organization in question truly able to provide what you need?
4. **Character**: This essential speaks to how the person or organization is wired on the deepest levels. Do they possess the moral and personal qualities necessary for trust?
5. **Track Record**: The best predictor of the future is the past. What does the past say about what is likely to happen in the future?

Importantly, these essentials pertain to the formation of trust between both individuals and groups. They apply to interpersonal relationships, and they also apply to connections involving companies, organizations, governments, and more.

This session will explore the first two essentials of trust, beginning with . . .

Essential 1: Understanding

People open themselves to the possibility of trust when they feel understood. They take the first step toward trust when they believe an individual or an organization truly gets what they are feeling, what they need, and what they view as important.

This process involves listening, but it is more than listening. Any teacher or professor can tell you that just because a person hears what you are saying—just because they are physically in the same room and encounter the sound waves made by your voice—does not mean they are processing or engaging with your words in a meaningful way.

For that reason, the "understanding" essential of trust needs to include an element of mirroring. When others are able to reflect our own thoughts and needs back to us in a meaningful way, we feel understood. The door is opened for trust to grow.

Consider the following examples where the essential of understanding is missing in a relationship:

1. You explain to your boss why something isn't working. He just keeps telling you why it should work just fine and to keep doing it his way.
2. You try to get your spouse to see how they are hurting you or how you feel sometimes in the relationship, but they negate what you are saying.
3. You try to explain your symptoms to your doctor, but she rushes through the exam based on a predetermined time limit. You feel missed.
4. You are going through something significant and share your experiences with a friend, but that friend immediately says, "Oh, I know, the same thing happened to me when I . . "

Use the space below to "fix" each of the four situations described above. How could the offending party demonstrate understanding in a meaningful way?

1. _____

2. _____

3. _____

4. _____

Consider this summary from chapter 4 of the *Trust* book:

So there is our first building block of trust, being and feeling understood, whether it happens in relationships between individuals or in groups, or in some kind of business or consumer setting. Understanding has emotional, psychological, physical, and communication components. It is a lifelong skill that begins in infancy and develops throughout our lives as we grow more in being connected to others and their experience.

Figuring out when we ourselves are understood and when we are not is also a lifelong skill. It takes a lot of wisdom, as we are wired to need it and people can fake it well. . . . It takes time to reveal who people really are. . . . For now, just start noticing the people you feel really get you, understand you, and know what you experience. Notice the ones with whom you feel safe.

In your own words, how would you define "understanding" as an essential of trust? What does it mean for you to feel understood?

_____

_____

_____

_____

Who are some of the people who truly "get" you—people with whom you feel safe and known?

_____

_____

_____

_____

Essential 2: Motive

The second essential of trust moves beyond what others understand and focuses on *why* they do what they do. This is critical because it is entirely possible for you and me to encounter people or companies who understand us, yet do not care about meeting our needs. They are mostly motivated by their own needs, desires, or agenda. Worse, it's possible for us to encounter people or organizations who actively and intentionally use their understanding to harm or manipulate us.

As we seek to build trust and be worthy of trust, then, we must consider the motives of the other party or parties involved.

In your own words, how would you define "motive" as an essential ingredient of trust? What is it, and why is it important for building trust?

Consider these thoughts from chapter 5 of the *Trust* book:

> Real trust transcends "moral codes," or "duty codes," in a powerful way: Love. Care. Compassion. We all grow up learning moral codes such as, "You should share with your sister or friend. That's the right thing to do." But, at some point, we all break a few rules. Rules are not powerful enough. But love is. The addict knows he should not drink so much, but he does. Yet, when he realizes the pain his drinking causes his ten-year-old, his love is a more powerful restrainer than the "rule" of staying sober. Meaningful moral codes depend upon the "law of love." The law of empathy, as we saw, makes us understand someone, and the intent to do them good instead of harm puts that into actionable trust.

Jesus said that all the rules in the entire Bible can be summed up in the law of love: "'Love the Lord your God with all your heart and with all your soul and with all your mind.' This is the first and greatest commandment. And the second is like it: 'Love your neighbor as yourself.' All the Law and the Prophets hang on these two commandments'" (Matthew 22:37-40 NIV).

True love has the motive and intent of first doing no harm, but more than that, looking out for the good of the other person or party. It is about being "for" them as well as "for" ourselves. That way, they can know that we "have their back," so carelessness can begin and guardedness diminish.

When have you felt like an employee of a company truly had your interests in mind, rather than solely thinking of that company's interests?

_____

_____

_____

_____

Imagine you were seeking a contractor to renovate a major feature of your home. How would you determine whether that contractor understands you and your needs?

_____

_____

_____

_____

How would you evaluate that contractor's motives?

_____

_____

_____

_____

Let's look at the other side of the mirror. The essentials of understanding and motive are important for creating an atmosphere in which you can trust others. But they are also helpful tools that allow you and me to evaluate our own trustworthiness.

Take a moment to do just that as we wrap up the personal study portion of this session.

When it comes to personal relationships, how well are you able to understand the needs and desires of other people?

1   2   3   4   5   6   7   8   9   10

(Not well)   _(Very well)_

When have you experienced tension in a relationship because you failed to understand who the other person was and what they needed? What factors contributed to that failure?

_____

_____

_____

_____

Use the space below to list three relationships that are currently important
to you. How would you describe your motivations for maintaining and
developing each of those relationships?

1. _____

_____

2. _____

_____

3. _____

_____

GROUP DISCUSSION

Icebreaker

Choose one of the following questions to begin your group's discussion on "The Essentials of Trust (Part 1)."

- What's one of the most memorable meals you have enjoyed? What made it memorable?
  or
- What are some of the biggest wants or needs that motivate you each day?

Content Review

What ideas or principles did you find most interesting from chapters 4–5 of *Trust*?

_____

_____

_____

_____

What questions have been on your mind since reading those chapters? Or, what seemed confusing that you'd like to have resolved?

_____

_____

_____

_____

The first essential of trust is understanding. People cannot be convinced or argued or debated into extending trust. They aren't looking for persuasive information or an air-tight résumé when they determine whether a person or organization is trustworthy—not at first.

Instead, before trust can be established in any meaningful way, people need to feel understood. They need to believe the person or organization in question recognizes who they are and what they need. When those conditions are met, a seed of trust can be planted.

How would you explain "understanding" as an essential of trust to someone who had never been exposed to this material?

_____

_____

_____

_____

Turn to page 53 of the *Trust* book and read through the example of how Chick-fil-A demonstrates understanding with its customers.

When have you been surprised by an organization who seemed to "get" you in a meaningful way?

_____

_____

_____

_____

The second essential of trust is motive. This is the "Why?" question. Unfortunately, there are many negative or unhelpful motivations that drive interactions between people, and between individuals and corporations. Power. Control. Greed. Domination. Dislike. Any of these will choke out the roots of trust before it can grow.

Thankfully, there are other motivations that are neutral or positive—motivations that form a soil in which trust can flourish. Many people (and, yes, many companies) genuinely desire to help others; they are service oriented. Others are driven by a desire to see improvement in their communities or create a positive impact. Even money need not be a negative when it comes to motive. The exchange of goods and services can be a fine foundation for trust when not spoiled by avarice and greed. But it is always enhanced when the other party feels like the business has a desire to make the outcome meet the real needs of the customer.

Understanding what drives others—and what drives us—is a key to establishing trust.

What methods can we use to discern the motives of other people?

_____

_____

_____

_____

What about companies? Governments?

_____

_____

_____

_____

Work as a group to make a list of the largest and most influential organizations in your community. This could include businesses, churches, schools, government agencies, and more.

What are some of the main ways those organizations talk about their motives within your community? What do they say about their intentions?

_____

_____

_____

_____

To what degree do the actions of those organizations match with what they communicate about their motives?

_____

_____

_____

_____

Case Study

Thomas is in charge of recruiting and training volunteers for the children's ministry at his church. That ministry is relatively large, serving several hundred children every week from the nursery all the way up to high schoolers. For that reason, Thomas regularly conducts interviews with potential volunteers.

Today, Thomas is meeting with Randall, a thirty-something male who has been attending the church for several months but is not yet a member. The plan is for the two men to have coffee so that Thomas can hear Randall's story and assess different options for service in the ministry.

Thomas has not admitted it out loud, but he is uncertain about allowing Randall to volunteer at the church—at least in the children's ministry. For most of the morning, Thomas has been trying to put his finger on what makes him uncomfortable. He knows very little about Randall's personal life and what motivates him to want to volunteer. Is he just looking for a "position" of authority? Or looking to be admired as a "helpful" person? Seeking accolades? Is he in it just to "have fun"?

At the same time, Thomas is aware of the responsibility he carries to make sure his volunteers are seeking to do the best thing for the children and their families, giving them the best experience possible. He wants volunteers to have a deep desire to help the children. He has also learned to trust his instincts.

Thomas is hoping the uncomfortable feeling in his gut will be resolved after his coffee and conversation with Randall. If it is not resolved, he will need to make some difficult decisions.

What factors make the need for trust especially important in this scenario?

_____

_____

_____

What are some feelings or desires Thomas is hoping to see mirrored in Randall during their conversation?

_____

_____

_____

How does a person's "gut" play into questions involving trust or the lack of trust? How should it apply to those questions?

_____

_____

_____

If you were in Thomas's place, what methods could you use to highlight or uncover Randall's motive in this scenario?

_____

_____

_____

_____

The final three essentials of trust are ability, character, and track record. Which of those feels most pertinent to Thomas's dilemma in this scenario? Why?

_____

_____

_____

_____

Wrap Up

Remember these truths as you conclude this discussion of session 2:

- Understanding is the first step in building trust. We are more likely to trust when someone learns what we like, what we need, what we want—and what hurts us.
- Motive is the second essential for building trust. Once understanding has been established, trust can continue to grow when others are motivated in ways that make us feel comfortable.
- Questions of trust go beyond interpersonal relationships and apply to all areas of our lives.

What is one action you would like to take this week based on what you've learned?

_____

_____

_____

_____

Let not mercy and truth forsake you;

Bind them around your neck,

Write them on the tablet of your heart,

And so find favor and high esteem

In the sight of God and man.

Trust in the Lord with all your heart,

And lean not on your own understanding;

In all your ways acknowledge Him,

And He shall direct your paths.

— Proverbs 3:3–6 NKJV

THE ESSENTIALS OF TRUST (PART 2)

In this session, you will:

- Explore the third essential of trust: ability.
- Explore the fourth essential of trust: character.
- Explore the fifth essential of trust: track record.
- Join with others to review these themes and discuss how they apply to your lives and your community.

Prior to engaging this session, read chapters 6–8 in the *Trust* trade book.

Personal Study

"Trust me."

When you hear those words, the concept can seem so simple. Sometimes it feels as if trust should be something we turn on and off like a light switch. "I choose to trust this person, I choose not to trust that person," and so on.

In reality, genuine trust is a complex process that requires many factors and many layers to develop. We are focused on five of those factors that research has highlighted as being of primary importance for the formation of trust. These are the essentials of trust.

The first essential is understanding. In order for trust to develop, people must believe the other party knows who they are and what they value. The second essential is motive. When individuals or organizations are motivated by something other than self-interest—and especially when those motivations serve a higher purpose—they create fertile ground for the growth of trust.

This session will explore the third, fourth, and fifth essentials of trust, beginning with . . .

Essential 3: Ability

In many situations, trust is a targeted experience. We're not looking to trust simply for the experience of trusting. Instead, we trust people or organizations to *do* something or *perform* in a specific way.

For example, when you hire a company to manage the lawn care around your home, you are not seeking companionship. You're not choosing a friend or a mentor or a counselor. You're hiring someone to do yard work. For that reason, besides making sure they understand your needs and have motives to serve you well, you will also take the time to identify whether that person or that company possesses the ability to perform that work well.

Notice there are two parts to this essential of trust. The first is ability. Is the party in question able to do what you expect or need them to do? Do they have the necessary skills, training, and experience? Do they own the right equipment? Do they have what it takes to come through when you place your trust in them?

The second is capacity, which refers to questions of time and stability. Continuing the example above, you could find the most skilled individual in your county to maintain your landscaping, but if he or she does not have any room in their schedule, or a large enough staff to take you on as a client, then trust would be fruitless. They lack capacity.

The bottom line is that you need understanding and motive to be supported by ability and capacity in order for trust to flourish.

Using your own words, how would you describe ability and capacity as an essential element of trust?

_____

_____

_____

_____

When have you learned the hard way that people or companies can have good motives but lack the necessary ability to provide what you need?

_____

_____

_____

_____

Consider this summary from chapter 6 of the *Trust* book:

> Think about the following situation. Someone falls "in love" with a great, honest, fun person. After a period of dating bliss, they hit the "trust button" and enter into marriage. But marriage takes more than love, honesty, and fun. There are some very important "abilities" required to make it work. Does this person have the ability to communicate, to resolve conflict, to be resilient under stress, to be a good mother or father to your future children, and to be financially responsible? How many marriages have you seen struggle or fail because these "abilities" were absent? Yet people frequently entrust

their entire lives to people who don't have the ability to be a good spouse, wrongly thinking they will be able to deliver on the marriage contract.

Where do you notice tension caused by a lack of ability in your closest relationships?

_____

_____

_____

_____

Essential 4: Character

The fourth essential of trust looks at the way people and organizations are wired. It explores their internal makeup, which I refer to as character.

Importantly, the concept of character goes beyond honesty and dishonesty. Certainly, honesty is bedrock. Nothing erodes or eliminates trust faster than deception. But whether a person lies is only one element or aspect of that person's character. There are many more elements, and there are many honest people who are not good candidates for trust because of other deficiencies.

We talk a lot about morality and goodness, but there is no "one size fits all" definition of character. Many in the leadership literature speak of emotional intelligence (EQ) or soft skills, and these can be helpful guides for exploring specific aspects of a person's internal makeup. The Bible also contains several passages that explore key elements of personal character from both a positive and negative perspective, and their relevance to trust.

Here is an example:

I hate what faithless people do;

I will have no part in it.

The perverse of heart shall be far from me;

I will have nothing to do with what is evil.

Whoever slanders their neighbor in secret,

I will put to silence;

whoever has haughty eyes and a proud heart,

I will not tolerate.

My eyes will be on the faithful in the land,

that they may dwell with me;

the one whose walk is blameless

will minister to me.

No one who practices deceit

will dwell in my house;

no one who speaks falsely

will stand in my presence.

— Psalm 101:3–7 NIV

In your experience, what are some key personal qualities that determine whether someone has trustworthy character?

_____

_____

_____

_____

What personal traits or characteristics are most important for you when it comes to establishing trust? In which specific contexts?

_____

_____

_____

_____

In the same way, what are some negative character traits that are trust "deal breakers"? In which specific contexts?

_____

_____

_____

_____

Specificity is an important consideration for this topic, as I made clear in this excerpt from chapter 7 of the *Trust* book:

> A person's trustworthiness is specific to the certain areas in which we trust them. Keeping this in mind will help keep us from being too perfectionistic about trust. We don't need someone to be perfect in every area of their makeup. We all have strengths, weaknesses, and deficiencies. We can accept and value a person in the midst of what they do not do well. The important question is *can they do what we need them to do for that context?* This is where trust either gets built, or dinged.
>
> When we realize this, we can love and appreciate someone for their strengths and in spite of their weaknesses or deficiencies. In a marriage where the couple values each other for their differences, you

will hear each partner laughing at what the other one does not possess. "Are you kidding? Send him to pick up all of the ingredients we need for the party?" The wife may say, "No way. He is too scattered and forgetful, and he would come home with only half of what's on the list. I need him to be here and greet guests because he makes every-one feel included and happy to be here. But I can't trust him to get the list right. I'll do that." And then they both laugh.

What options do we have for evaluating a person's character? How can we determine their strengths and weaknesses?

_____

_____

_____

_____

What about a company or an organization?

_____

_____

_____

_____

Essential 5: Track Record

The fifth essential of trust is the track record a person or organization brings to the table. This essential is the easiest to understand in terms of a definition, although separating fact from fiction can be a challenge when it comes to actually reviewing a specific track record.

When I say "track record," I simply mean what has happened in the past. Why focus on past events? Because what an individual or an organization *has* done is the best indicator of what they *will* do. Not a perfect indicator, mind you. People and circumstances can change. But in general, unless something has changed, the past is a great predictor of the future.

The practical truth here is that promises mean little when it comes to trust. What people say they will do means little; what they have done means a lot. The same is true for individuals and organizations who apologize for past mistakes. Apologies are good and *can* be an indicator of a desire for change. But actual change in behavior is needed before trust can be extended.

Imagine your child is sick at school, and you can't get there for several hours. Who would you call to help? (If you don't have a child, imagine your car broke down on a lonely road and you need assistance.) List the five people you would ask for help, starting with those you'd call first.

1. _____

2. _____

3. _____

4. _____

5. _____

Look at the first two names listed above. In what way do those people have a positive track record for dealing with such a crisis?

_____

_____

_____

_____

What are effective steps we can take to evaluate the track record of a person?

_____

_____

_____

As we prepare to wrap up this exploration of the five essentials of trust, let's look again at the other side of the mirror. You have strengths and weaknesses when it comes to your ability within relationships (and as a professional). You have a unique character. And you have a track record that others will use to extrapolate how you are most likely to behave in the present and the future.

Each of those realities will play into the decisions others make when deciding whether to trust you.

In what areas of your life have you demonstrated a strong ability that would encourage others to trust you? What are your strengths?

_____

_____

_____

_____

When have people said that you lack something important that hindered their ability to trust or connect with you?

_____

_____

_____

What are some words that describe your character? How are you wired on the inside?

_____

_____

_____

_____

In terms of personal relationships with family, friends, and coworkers, what would you point to as evidence that you have a track record worthy of trust? In what areas?

_____

_____

_____

_____

GROUP DISCUSSION

Icebreaker

Choose one of the following questions to begin your group's discussion on "The Essentials of Trust (Part 2)."

- On a scale of 1 (low) to 10 (high), how would you rate your ability to "read" people during a first meeting?
  or
- When have you recently felt motivated to post a review online? Why?

Content Review

What ideas or principles did you find most interesting from chapters 6–8 of *Trust*?

_____

_____

_____

_____

What questions have been on your mind since reading those chapters?
Or, what seemed confusing that you'd like to have resolved?

_____

_____

_____

_____

When understanding and motive move in a positive direction, the ground is prepared for the third essential of trust: ability. This is the "How?" question. How will the other party hold up their end of the bargain if trust is offered? Are they able to do what you are asking them to do?

This is important because it's possible for someone to understand what you need and be motivated by a genuine desire to meet your need—yet not be able to do so. They lack skills or resources necessary for establishing trust in a specific context. Or, they lack the capacity; they simply don't have the time or emotional stability to provide what you need when you need it.

In other words, people or companies may be trustworthy in general ways, but not trustworthy in the *specific* way that lines up with your specific needs.

In your own words, why is ability a necessary ingredient for trust?

_____

_____

_____

_____

Turn to page 75 in the *Trust* book and read the story of Bradley, the COO turned CEO. The board made the mistake of not properly evaluating Bradley's ability because they already trusted him. How do similar mistakes show up in our personal relationships?

_____

_____

_____

_____

The fourth essential of trust is character. This refers to our internal makeup—moral qualities, emotional intelligence, personal traits, and more. We are born with many aspects of our personal makeup. They come from the DNA that determines our height, weight, and hair color. However, character is something that grows and develops over time, and while inborn temperaments are influencers of parts of our makeup, character is much more complex than what we are "born with." Life and experience have a powerful way of shaping and shifting who we are as we grow and develop.

When it comes to the issue of trust, we will generally be rewarded when we invest trust in people and organizations with strong character—those whose moral and personal qualities align with our own and move in a positive direction.

What standards can be used to determine whether an individual or company has a strong character? What standards should be used?

_____

_____

_____

_____

How would you describe the difference between character and motive?

_____

_____

_____

_____

The fifth and final essential of trust is track record. Any time we extend trust to another person or to an organization, we are exposing ourselves to risk. We are becoming vulnerable by relying on something outside of ourselves. If the other party does not prove worthy of our trust, we will be harmed in some way—emotionally, financially, spiritually, relationally, and so on. Broken trust always produces consequences.

Track record is a way of mitigating those potential consequences. When a person or company has shown the ability to come through for us or for others in the past, we can feel more confident that they will come through in the present and the future. Therefore, we are more likely to extend trust.

When has the track record of a person or company convinced you not to trust them? What specifically made you nervous?

_____

_____

_____

_____

What are some factors that often cause us to ignore track record when we are considering whether to extend trust?

_____

_____

_____

_____

Case Study

As a group, spend fifteen to thirty minutes watching commercials. These can be advertisements currently playing on TV or through streaming services, or they can be commercials you remember from the past.

After watching each commercial, talk through the following questions to discuss how that particular advertisement appeals to different essentials of trust. (Note: It's likely that a given commercial will not appeal to every essential of trust. So, the answer to some of the questions below may be "None" or "It doesn't.")

In what ways does this commercial appeal to the ability essential of trust? (How is the company attempting to show its abilities in a positive way?)

_____

_____

_____

_____

In what ways does this commercial appeal to the character essential of trust? (How is the company attempting to highlight a strong or positive character?)

_____

_____

_____

_____

In what ways does this commercial appeal to the track record essential of trust? (How is the company trying to establish a strong record from the past?)

_____

_____

_____

_____

After you have watched all the commercials, finish by discussing these questions:

In your opinion, which commercial did the best job of establishing firm ground for a trust relationship with potential clients? Why? What aspects of any of the five essentials of trust connected with you?

_____

_____

_____

_____

In a more general sense, how can we avoid being fooled by companies that do not deserve our trust?

_____

_____

_____

_____

How can we avoid being fooled by individuals who do not deserve our trust?

_____

_____

_____

_____

Wrap Up

Remember these truths as you conclude this discussion of session 3:

- Ability is the third essential of trust. We need to feel confident in the skills, abilities, resources, and experiences of a potential connection.
- Character is the fourth essential of trust. When a person (or company) offers a strong internal makeup that aligns with our values, we are more likely to trust. Also, we need to make sure their "makeup" can bring to us what we are going to need in that context, or we will feel let down.
- Track record is the fifth essential of trust. What a person or company has done in the past is the best indicator of what they will do in the future.

What is one action you would like to take this week based on what you've learned?

_____

_____

_____

_____

For this very reason, make every effort to add to your faith virtue; and to virtue, knowledge; and to knowledge, self-control; and to self-control, perseverance; and to perseverance, godliness; and to godliness, brotherly kindness; and to brotherly kindness, love.

— 2 Peter 1:5–7 BSB

BUILDING TRUST MUSCLES

In this session, you will:

- Learn the concept of "trust muscles" and their role in our ability to give and receive trust.
- Explore different types of barriers that often hinder our ability to trust.
- Explore specific fears and traumas that create such barriers.
- Join with others to review these themes and discuss how they apply to your lives and your community.

Prior to engaging this session, read chapters 9–11 in the *Trust* trade book.

Personal Study

You don't have to be a body builder to understand how muscles grow and develop. When you put strain on your biceps, for example, whether through weight lifting or regular use, the fibers in those muscles break down. They are damaged by exertion and moving past their comfortable present capacity. Then, as your body works to repair those fibers, it naturally adds a little extra protection to prevent further damage. It adds new muscle tissue, and so your muscles grow.

Stop for a moment and consider the wonders of our human frames! We are designed not only to survive the trials and exertions of everyday life, but to thrive in them. To grow through them. This is a gift.

There is a similar dynamic at play when it comes to the essential element of life we call trust. Trusting others takes work. It requires effort. Not to mention that making ourselves vulnerable enough to trust means opening ourselves to the very real risk of harm. That's the scarier news.

The good news is that the more we do the work of building and maintaining trust, the stronger our "trust muscles" become. We can grow and develop in our ability to trust.

This is important because, in the same way people develop different musculature because of genetics and life experiences, we don't all grow into adulthood with the same ability to trust. There are differences in the size and strength of our trust muscles, which is why some trust more easily (and more effectively) than others.

Even so, any individual can grow in their ability to trust meaningfully and effectively.

Use the following scale to measure your natural ability to trust. How easy do you find it to trust others on a day-to-day basis?

1   2   3   4   5   6   7   8   9   10

(Very difficult)   *(Very easy)*

What are some specific ways you would like to grow and develop in your ability to trust? Where do you want to improve your trust muscles?

_____

_____

_____

_____

Past experiences are one of the biggest factors that influence our ability to trust in the present. Perhaps the biggest. If we have been rewarded in the past because our trust in others resulted in great blessings—trust in our parents, for example—then we will likely find it easier to trust in our current relationships. We will be conditioned to trust.

But if our past experiences with trust caused damage in our lives, we will likely have difficulty trusting others in the present. And in the future. Perhaps trust muscles never developed because loving caregivers never appeared. Perhaps those muscles are atrophied from lack of use. Or, perhaps our trust muscles are broken because of betrayals that were never healed.

In these circumstances, developing new strength in those trust muscles will require dealing with the pain of the past.

Read through Sean's story on pages 123–133 of the *Trust* book. What emotions do you experience as you engage that story? Why?

_____

_____

_____

_____

What are some of the main moments from your past in which trust was strained? Even broken?

_____

_____

_____

_____

Consider these thoughts from page 131 of the *Trust* trade book:

> Trust muscles can be repaired. An old issue that replays itself in someone's life can be healed in the present. Had Sean been open, he could have gotten over his dad's mistreatment, and it would not have continued to cause him to fear authority and accountability. He could have realized that other people in authority are different than his dad. He could have learned to notice how he misinterpreted the present because of his past and developed some new responses and other skills that would have changed his life. This would have occurred in the present with some good help, but it did have roots in the past.
>
> Not recognizing how we taint the present and distort it based on our past experience is the essence of failing to learn and grow. At some point, we do well to learn: "Yes, it was cold in January and you needed that overcoat. Now it is June, and you'd feel better if you took it off." We no longer need the defensive behaviors against trust that we learned in the past. Instead, we need to learn to grow "past our past." We need new skills, and new trust equipment, which can be built in new, more secure relationships.

Think of a moment from the past when fear caused you to run away from an opportunity to trust—a time when you "wore your overcoat in June." This may have been a relationship, a business opportunity, or even something as simple as making a purchase. What are some different ways you could have responded in that moment?

_____

_____

_____

_____

Attachment theory is a popular concept in counseling and psychology circles. According to that theory, our interactions with our parents and other caregivers during childhood have a lasting impact on our ability to form and maintain relationships. This includes our ability to give and receive trust.

Research around this theory suggests people often fit into one or more "attachment styles," which are broad patterns of behavior. Gaining a firm understanding of those styles can be helpful as we seek to develop our trust muscles.

Review the four attachment styles listed on pages 136–139 of the *Trust* book, then answer the questions that follow.

How would you summarize or define each attachment style in your own words?

The secure attachment style:

_____

_____

_____

The anxious attachment style:

_____

_____

_____

The avoidant attachment style:

_____

_____

_____

The fearful-avoidant attachment style:

_____

_____

_____

Which attachment style fits you best? Why?

_____

_____

_____

My point in emphasizing these themes is that wanting to build your trust muscles may not be enough. Choosing to grow in your ability to trust may not be as simple as it sounds.

If past events are hindering your ability to trust in the here and now, you may need to address them before your ability to trust improves. If your trust muscles are damaged or atrophied, they will likely need significant healing before they can once again bear the full weight of genuine trust and vulnerability. That is the reality you may face.

Thankfully, healing is possible. I know that from my own experiences and from my work as a counselor. Your ability to trust can be restored, and your trust muscles can grow.

We will explore several steps for doing that good work over the next three sessions. First, however, I'd like you to walk through a quick exercise designed to help you stretch your trust muscles a little bit.

Take a moment to think of an action connected to trust that would make you feel slightly uncomfortable. For example, if you don't typically share your emotions with other people, you could talk with your spouse (or a friend) and do just that—talk through a recent occasion in which you felt strong emotions. Or, if you have a strained (or apathetic) relationship with one of your parents, call him or her and strive to achieve a positive conversation.

The goal is to do something that stretches your trust muscles. But only a stretch! Don't dive into a situation that is likely to create a high amount of pain, reinjury, stress, or strain. Use the questions below to complete the exercise.

What do you plan to do as a trust-muscle stretch?

_____

_____

_____

_____

How did it go? What was positive? What was negative?

_____

_____

_____

_____

GROUP DISCUSSION

Icebreaker

Choose one of the following questions to begin your group's discussion on "Building Trust Muscles."

- If you could enjoy only one form of exercise for the rest of your life, which would you choose? Why?
  or
- What are some words you would use to describe your relationship with your father, or mother?

Content Review

What ideas or principles did you find most interesting from chapters 9–11 of *Trust*?

_____

_____

_____

What questions have been on your mind since reading those chapters? Or, what seemed confusing that you'd like to have resolved?

_____

_____

_____

_____

Earlier in this study, we explored the five essentials of trust: understanding, motive, ability, character, and track record. These are the critical factors that, when met, create a safe environment for us to become vulnerable and take the risks associated with trust.

Importantly, though, we must remember that trust is a two-way street. A trust relationship always involves two parties. So, even when we encounter an individual or an organization that seems trustworthy, we still have work to do. We still have a decision to make.

Namely, will we take the step and choose to trust—or will we shrink back?

When the latter occurs, it could be a sign that we are the problem. Likely we will need to restore or rehabilitate our ability to trust. Our "trust muscles."

What are some ways "trust muscles" are similar to physical muscles? What are some ways they are different?

_____

_____

_____

_____

_____

When have you seen someone be harmed or held back because of "trust issues"?

_____

_____

_____

_____

_____

Where have you possibly missed out on an opportunity because of "trust issues"?

_____

_____

_____

_____

What steps can we take to evaluate our ability to trust? (How do we measure or test our trust muscles?)

_____

_____

_____

_____

Fear is a major barrier to trust. In fact, fear is likely the biggest obstacle that prevents us from extending trust in situations where trust is warranted.

Sometimes it's the fear of depending on other people. We could not help depending on other people when we were children. Little ones are always helpless. Always vulnerable. Therefore, if our caregivers acted in ways that caused us pain or left us feeling abandoned, we can develop a serious fear of repeating that same pattern as adults. We become afraid of vulnerability.

On the flip side, sometimes we are afraid of people *requiring* us to depend on them. If our parents or caregivers constantly hovered over us and involved themselves in every area of our lives, we can develop a resistance to anything that feels similar. We develop a fear of being controlled.

Oftentimes we resist establishing trust because we don't want others to see the "real me." We are afraid of uncovering our weaknesses. Even our shame or failures.

And, when we have experienced any significant type of trauma, we can be terrorized by triggers that remind us of that past damage.

For all these reasons and more, learning to develop our trust muscles often requires us to face our fears.

Review the "attachment styles" content from pages 136–139 of the *Trust* trade book. What did you learn about yourself by reading that material?

_____

_____

_____

_____

Take a small step in exercising your trust muscles by talking about your fears within your group. Identify something from your past that has caused you to act fearfully in the present, and then share those experiences with the group. How has that fear impacted your ability to trust?

_____

_____

_____

_____

Case Study

Sandy is excited to start her new job as publisher of a well-known brand in a large and established publishing company. There's lots to like about the job. Good pay. Great benefits. Sandy will have access to more resources than she did in previous positions because of the size of her new publishing company. Best of all, Sandy will be the primary boss of her team. She will be able to manage and shape that team as she sees fit.

The bad news is that Sandy's predecessor was a nightmare of a leader. The previous publisher was vindictive and temperamental. He had been part of the company for decades, which meant he knew all the power players and took little accountability for his actions. He considered himself untouchable and became a tyrant.

While that publisher was eventually dismissed, the team of sixteen supporting employees suffered through several painful years. As a result, many of them are considering retirement or finding new jobs. Others have learned to keep their heads down and never do anything that might spark a reaction from the boss. The workplace has been deeply unhealthy, and the workers themselves don't know how to change.

Sandy will need to rebuild the camaraderie of her team and reestablish a healthy working environment for everyone involved.

If you were one of the workers on Sandy's team, what fears might you be wrestling with as you prepare to meet a new boss?

_____

_____

_____

_____

In your opinion, would it be appropriate or helpful for Sandy to "call out" the harmful behavior of her predecessor as she engages with the team? Why or why not?

_____

_____

_____

_____

What are some possible steps Sandy could take to establish herself as a leader worthy of trust?

What are some small steps she could take to help her new teammates exercise their trust muscles?

Wrap Up

Remember these truths as you conclude this discussion of session 4:

- Trust is a two-way street. Even when others prove worthy of trust, we still must choose to accept the risk of extending that trust.
- We all have "trust muscles" that allow us to do the work of trust. These muscles can grow and develop through the right growth and exercise routine.
- Part of developing our trust muscles is learning to address the fears and traumas of the past that make it difficult to trust in the present.

What is one action you would like to take this week based on what you've learned?

Be on your guard; stand firm in the faith; be courageous; be strong.

Do everything in love.

— 1 Corinthians 16:13–14 NIV

REPAIRING TRUST (PART 1)

In this session, you will:

- Take a broad look at the issue of rebuilding trust after a betrayal.
- Explore the first step for repairing trust: *heal from what happened to you.*
- Explore the second step for repairing trust: *move beyond anger and revenge and turn toward forgiveness.*
- Join with others to review these themes and discuss how they apply to your lives and your community.

Prior to engaging this session, read chapters 12–14 in the *Trust* trade book.

Personal Study

"Can I ever trust again?"

It's a question that has been asked far too many times by far too many people. The pain inherent in that question illustrates both the necessity of trust as a foundational element in our lives and the reality that broken trust is an especially bitter experience.

I've walked with hundreds of clients as they wrestled through that question and everything it implies. That list includes spouses, parents, siblings, coworkers, board members, and more. People of every stripe and circumstance are forced to deal with the repercussions of broken trust—not to mention the questions that come with it.

"Can I trust her?" "*Should* I trust him?" "What will happen if we trust them?" "How could I ever move forward?"

Thankfully, such questions have answers. Choosing to trust again is just that: a choice. But it's not a decision we have to make based only on gut feelings or depending on crystal balls. We don't have to guess whether a person or company is worthy of a second chance.

Instead, we can look for specific, objective qualities that, when present, open the door for a renewed opportunity to trust. In my experience, the best way to seek out those qualities is to follow a six-step process:

1. Heal from what happened to you.
2. Move beyond anger and revenge and turn toward forgiveness.
3. Ponder what you really want.
4. Figure out if reconciliation is available.
5. Assess trustworthiness to determine if trust is an option.
6. Look for evidence of real change.

When have you been forced to evaluate the question "Can I trust again?"

_____

_____

With the benefit of hindsight, what did you do well in determining whether or not to give the other party a second chance?

_____

_____

_____

What mistakes did you make in that process?

_____

_____

_____

_____

What are your first impressions of the six steps for rebuilding trust listed above?

_____

_____

_____

_____

One clarification: While I've presented the six steps above in a numbered list, that doesn't mean we will experience them in a linear fashion. We won't always move from step 1 to step 2, and from step 4 to step 5. Repairing trust is not neat and tidy; therefore, we may bounce around from step to step (circling through or repeating steps) during the process.

In this session, we will explore the first two steps in that process, starting with…

Step 1: Heal from What Happened to You

When you experience the pain of betrayal or broken trust, the very first thing to do is to seek healing. And this step may take some time and work.

How much time? There's no way to tell. Every person is unique, and so is every situation in which trust needs to be restored. In a general sense, bigger betrayals will require more time and more resources for healing. But there is no "one size fits all" formula for determining how long you will need before you can evaluate your options from a healthy place.

Consider this directive from page 174 of the *Trust* trade book:

Whether personal or professional, the first step toward healing is always this: **connect with people you feel safe with and supported by, and let them help**. Don't isolate or withdraw or think you can be strong enough to heal by yourself. Even Navy SEALs need their buddies in times of battle. The people you connect with may be close friends, a therapist, a couples' counselor, a mentor, or a prayer group. If the betrayal is professional, you may also connect with a board of directors or lead investors in a business, trusted advisers, or your team at work (if appropriate). Other people bring valuable resources to your situation, resources that can help you get stable and healed. You need them to support and care for you, and you need their wisdom and the ability to help you figure out next steps. Support and wisdom are vital.

Allowing people to support you, care for you, and share their wisdom as you heal helps move you beyond the initial shock, numbness, denial, and catastrophic thinking that interferes with judgment, so you can process the pain. Even in a business setting, these emotions and thinking issues run rampant. I have seen high-level business leaders sustain betrayals by significant trusted parties and walk the same path emotionally as a jilted spouse or lover. Trust is a bond, an attachment, and no matter whether a breach of trust happens in a personal relationship or a business context, it can strike the heart the same way. So, the pain and wound require processing and time to bleed off the emotions. This will help you become strong enough to move into the next step.

When was the last time you experienced a significant physical injury? How long did it take you to heal completely?

_____

_____

_____

What are some cues our bodies give us to show that we have recovered from a physical injury? What are some cues that we are not fully recovered?

_____

_____

_____

What are some possible cues that can reveal we are ready to move forward from the mental and emotional damage of betrayal?

_____

_____

_____

What are some possible risks of moving forward or making decisions too quickly after trust has been broken?

_____

_____

_____

Step 2: Move Beyond Anger and Revenge and Turn Toward Forgiveness

For most people, the sting of betrayal narrows the focus to a single train of thought: anger. When we've been hurt, it's easy to wallow in anger or even the desire to hurt back. We sometimes want the offending party to feel the same pain we've been forced to deal with, and so we cry out with Sir Walter Scott: "Revenge, the sweetest morsel to the mouth that ever was cooked in hell." (Gross, but a common feeling.)

Such thoughts are common and perhaps natural. But they are not helpful. It is forgiveness, not vengeance or even holding on too long to anger, that offers the only real path to free yourself from betrayal.

How easy do you find it to forgive others when they hurt you or cross boundaries in your life?

1   2   3   4   5   6   7   8   9   10

(Very difficult)   *(Very easy)*

In your experience, what are some dangers inherent with refusing to forgive others?

_____

_____

_____

_____

There are two important clarifications that we need to examine when it comes to forgiving those who betray us.

First, forgiving someone does not mean foregoing emotions. When we choose to forgive, we don't pretend nothing happened; we don't ignore the reality of what was done to us. For that reason, forgiveness does not require us to ignore the emotional damage that is intricately connected with betrayal. The emotions are part of the process.

As I wrote on page 181 of the *Trust* book:

Resolving anger is one of the biggest aspects of forgiveness. It is essential to the process, in both directions: *you must have anger to get better, and at some point you must give up the anger to get better.* By "have anger" I mean that to forgive someone, you have to be honest about blaming them. They are guilty. Period. They did something harmful or painful to you. You cannot deny what they have done and expect to forgive them well. Forgiveness requires a wrong. So call the wrong what it is, and name it. Be honest about it. And know that doing so will lead to a period of anger. So, face the fact that you are angry about it. . . .

Anger is an emotion that says "something is wrong." It is a protest emotion, meaning that it gears up the system for action to fight something that is wrong. So, if there has been a betrayal, you are likely going to be angry about it. That is okay and good. The issue is how you handle your anger and what you do with it. It can be destructive, or it can be a force for good.

One of my favorite verses is Ephesians 4:26: Be angry, but "in your anger do not sin" (NIV). God designed the human system to emotionally protest injustice. Allow yourself to feel and express anger, but don't do anything destructive in the process. Don't act it out; talk it out.

How do you typically handle the emotion of anger? Do you act out, bury it, or something else?

_____

_____

_____

_____

_____

Think of a situation that is currently causing you to feel angry. What would it look life for you to be angry, but "in your anger do not sin"?

_____

_____

_____

_____

    The second clarification is that offering forgiveness is not the same thing as a renewed offering of trust. Forgiving a person who has betrayed you does not mean you are required to extend that person a second chance.

    Here is the basic principle: forgiveness should be free, but trust must be earned. This is especially true in a situation where trust was broken and needs to be restored.

When have you experienced the consequences of holding on to anger for too long? What happened?

_____

_____

_____

_____

When has not giving yourself permission to be angry hurt you in some way?

_____

_____

_____

_____

In your words, what does it mean to "forgive" someone who has betrayed your trust? What steps are involved in that process?

_____

_____

_____

GROUP DISCUSSION

Icebreaker

Choose one of the following questions to begin your group's discussion on "Repairing Trust (Part 1)."

- When was the last time you successfully built something or repaired something in your home? What are some words you would use to describe that experience?

  or

- If you could choose any place in the world to spend a month solely focused on resting and healing, where would you go? What would you do?

Content Review

What ideas or principles did you find most interesting from chapters 12–14 of *Trust*?

_____

_____

What questions have been on your mind since reading those chapters?
Or, what seemed confusing that you'd like to have resolved?

_____

_____

_____

_____

When it comes to repairing trust, one of the most important things we can remember is that such a repair takes time. If rebuilding trust is possible, it will always be a process—never something that happens by simply flipping a switch in our minds and hearts.

Part of that process will involve the five essentials of trust we explored at the beginning of this study: understanding, motive, ability, character, and track record. When trust has been broken, we can use these five essentials to evaluate our previous experiences with the party in question and determine whether or not that person has changed in ways that are positive.

Rebuilding trust can also involve strengthening our trust muscles, which we examined in the previous session. Even when the other person (or organization) has proven themselves worthy of a second chance, we may have work to do before we can extend trust once more. We may need to exercise and expand our ability to trust.

With those tools in place, we will spend the next three sessions (including this one) exploring a helpful road map for the process of rebuilding trust. That road map offers six important steps, although those steps will not always be linear—there will likely be some bouncing back and forth.

Here are those six steps:

1. Heal from what happened to you.
2. Move beyond anger and revenge and turn toward forgiveness.
3. Ponder what you really want.

4. Figure out if reconciliation is available.

5. Assess trustworthiness to determine if trust is an option.

6. Look for evidence of real change.

What surprises you about these six steps? Why?

_____

_____

_____

_____

In a situation where trust has been broken and could potentially be repaired, what are some specific ways the five essentials of trust can be applied to aid in that process?

_____

_____

_____

_____

The first step in rebuilding trust is to heal. Specifically, to take whatever time and space is necessary for your heart to heal from the damage it sustained. That may sound counterintuitive, but in my experience such healing is critical for many reasons.

Remember, any time we extend trust to another person or company, we are making ourselves vulnerable. We are placing ourselves at risk. Sometimes that risk is miniscule, such as purchasing a product from a company. In many situations, however, that risk is quite large. This is especially true in our most important or intimate relationships. For that reason, we need to regain our strength before we put ourselves at risk of more potential harm.

It's also true that we don't make great decisions when we are still recovering from pain. That is true of physical damage, but it is especially true when we are attempting to heal from mental and emotional pain.

As I wrote on page 174 of the *Trust* book:

> One of the main reasons you need these is that you can't even think well when you are significantly wounded. You will make bad choices. When you're in pain, the urge to withdraw, strike back, or make rash decisions is strong, especially if the betrayal is personal. The more your heart is involved, the greater the pain.

Review the story of Finley the dog on pages 172–173 of the *Trust* book. In terms of trust, when have you "jumped back in the pool" too quickly?

_____

_____

_____

_____

_____

What would it look like for you to set aside time and space to heal from a painful betrayal?

_____

_____

_____

_____

The second step in the process of repairing trust is to move away from anger and revenge, and to instead turn toward forgiveness. Once again, this may feel counterintuitive. When we've been hurt, the last thing we want to consider is forgiveness.

But we must. Why? Because unforgiveness is simply another form of betrayal—one we impose upon ourselves.

As I wrote on page 179 of the *Trust* book:

> Unforgiveness can turn you into a bitter, vengeful person. It causes you to lose aspects of your soul and life to the person who betrayed you. As long as you hold on to what wrong they did, they still own you. As I heard someone say once, "When you remain angry, you are just a character in someone else's story." When you let go and forgive, you are free to write your own story. You do not have to be worried about settling an old score.

Importantly, forgiveness is not the first step in this process of repairing trust. Start by taking the space necessary for healing, which includes giving yourself time to experience the real emotions of anger, hurt, bitterness, and even rage. Don't ignore those emotions or try to push them down. Feel them, process them, and work through them.

Eventually, though, you will need to make the choice to forgive. That is when you start setting yourself free.

What does it mean to forgive someone who has wronged us? What does it *not* mean?

_____

_____

_____

_____

_____

Where are you currently resisting an opportunity to forgive someone?
What is holding you back?

_____

_____

_____

_____

Case Study

Trevor feels like he is in the middle of a nightmare. One week ago, he discovered that his wife, Cindy, was having an affair with a coworker. That discovery came after Trevor noticed some strange texts on Cindy's phone, which caused him to investigate further. The affair had been going on for more than a year.

Today, Trevor came home to find divorce papers waiting for him on the kitchen table. Cindy left the papers with a note explaining all the reasons why she was choosing the other man, her coworker, over Trevor. She filed for a fast-moving divorce based on claims of emotional abuse and incompatibility.

Trevor and Cindy were married for almost ten years. They have two young children. Yet in a single week, everything has come crashing down. And Trevor has no idea what to do next.

In your opinion, what are some immediate and specific steps Trevor should take in the next two days? In the next two weeks?

_____

_____

_____

_____

What might it look like for Trevor to find time and space for healing after this
bombshell betrayal?

_____

_____

_____

_____

_____

How would you advise Trevor to deal with his emotions during this initial period?
What emotions should he be experiencing, and how can he process them?

_____

_____

_____

_____

_____

After Trevor has given himself time to heal, what might it look like for him to
extend forgiveness to Cindy?

_____

_____

_____

_____

_____

Wrap Up

Remember these truths as you conclude this discussion of session 5:

- Broken trust can be repaired; it is possible. However, successfully rebuilding trust after a betrayal requires a process.
- The first step in that process is for the wounded party to take whatever time and space is necessary for healing. Allow your heart to heal before even thinking about whether trust can be repaired.
- The second step in that process is to move away from anger and the desire for revenge, and to intentionally move toward forgiveness.

What is one action you would like to take this week based on what you've learned?

_____

_____

_____

_____

REPAIRING TRUST (PART 2)

In this session, you will:

- Explore the third step for repairing trust: *ponder what you really want.*
- Explore the fourth step for repairing trust: *figure out if reconciliation is available.*
- Join with others to review these themes and discuss how they apply to your lives and your community.

Prior to engaging this session, read chapters 15–16 in the *Trust* trade book.

Personal Study

"What would you like?"

It's a question we often consider in superficial situations. What restaurant would you like to try for dinner? What shoes would you like to pair with that outfit? What show would you like to watch this evening? Would you like fries with that?

This is not a problem. Much of our everyday lives revolve around routines filled with superficial decisions and shallow needs.

However, there are times when we must step outside of those routines and choose to go deeper. There are times when we need to reject the superficial world around us, focus internally on what's happening inside us, and take a profound look at that question: "What would I like?" *What do I want? What do I need?*

Choosing whether to rebuild trust after a betrayal is one of those times.

Think back to a time when you felt betrayed, or when trust was broken. What were the main areas of concern on your mind in the weeks and months after that betrayal?

_____

_____

_____

_____

With the benefit of hindsight, what did you need most in that season of deciding if you should move forward with that person?

_____

_____

_____

_____

As we saw in the previous session, the first two steps for repairing trust may feel a little counterintuitive: 1) take the time and space necessary to heal, and 2) move away from anger and revenge, and move toward forgiveness.

In this session, we will explore the next two steps in that process, starting with . . .

Step 3: Ponder What You Really Want

One of the reasons it can be so difficult to determine how to move forward after a betrayal is that doing so involves two bad options. If we choose not to repair trust, we are moving on from a relationship in which we have invested much—one that has produced many blessings. We may have to make additional tough choices about children, finances, friendships, and more.

That is painful.

If we choose to make an effort to repair a broken trust, we face a long and uncertain road in the future. We will have to work through the pain of that betrayal and answer agonizing questions about whether we can extend trust a second time. (Or a third time, or a fourth time, etc.) And we do all that with the knowledge that we may not find a fairy-tale ending. All our effort might be in vain.

That is also painful.

Given that reality, it's necessary that we invest time and energy working our way through possible scenarios for the future. What could happen if we make this choice? What could happen if we make that choice? What is the best-case scenario? What about worst-case? What do I stand to lose, or gain?

As I wrote on page 192 of the *Trust* book:

> More often than not, pondering what you want is an unfolding process. Sometimes you can't know what you want until you have engaged in some of the steps we'll look at in later chapters because you don't really know if that person is changing or not. You don't yet know who you are dealing with—Jekyll, Hyde, or someone (hopefully) new. Don't feel you have to have it all figured out right now. But do begin the process of pondering what you really want so you will have a direction moving forward.

Take a moment to practice determining what you want by identifying some major goals for your life.

What are your primary life goals for this year? What do you want to accomplish or experience?

_____

_____

_____

What are your primary life goals for the next five years?

_____

_____

_____

The next twenty-five years?

_____

_____

_____

Which of your deepest relationships are currently helping you move toward those goals?

_____

_____

_____

_____

Which of your relationships (with people or organizations) are pushing you further from those goals?

_____

_____

_____

_____

Step 4: Figure Out If Reconciliation Is Available

As we move to step 4 in the process of repairing trust, it's important to emphasize that there are more than two categories for your relationships. People don't exist simply as "trusted" or "not trusted." There is a range—a spectrum that spans different levels of connection based on different experiences and interactions.

This spectrum still exists in situations where trust has been broken and may possibly be repaired. For that reason, we don't move someone from the "not trusted" category all the way to "fully trusted" in one jump. There is a series of stages those people should move through in the process of repairing trust.

We've already explored one of those stages, which is forgiving. That is step 2 in this process of repairing trust. After a betrayal, you have the power to forgive the person or organization who hurt you. You can extend that forgiveness on your own, without any sign of remorse or apology from the other party. And you should, because forgiveness sets _you_ free, not them.

The next stage is reconciling, which is the focus of step 4. To be clear, reconciling with someone who broke your trust does not mean fully trusting that person again—not yet. It simply means the other party has recognized their fault, accepted responsibility, and apologized. For that reason, you are able to return that relationship to a place of, at least, cordiality and positive interaction.

Reconciliation is akin to becoming non-conflictual once more with the person who betrayed you. But it is not officially extending trust.

Review the section called "Determine Who You're Dealing With" on pages 196–199 of the *Trust* trade book. In your own words, what is the difference between "forgiveness" and "reconciliation"?

_____

_____

_____

_____

What is the difference between "reconciliation" and "trust"?

_____

_____

_____

_____

The book highlights three types of people we may encounter in situations requiring reconciliation. How would you describe each type in your own words?

Wise People:

_____

_____

_____

_____

Fools or Mockers:

_____

_____

_____

_____

Evildoers:

_____

_____

_____

_____

Let's take a moment to look at the other side of the mirror, because reconciliation often requires effort from both parties. Meaning, in situations where trust is broken, it is also good for the one who was betrayed to look at how they would be smart to grow as well, learning from the experience. Even in circumstances where one party is obviously the one in the wrong, the betrayed one can learn as well.

Even when you are the one betrayed, it is good to figure out what growth steps the whole experience surfaced for you.

To admit that you have some things to learn does not mean you are the problem. It does not mean in any way your actions or attitudes caused the betrayal. That responsibility lies on the one who did the betrayal. Instead, choosing to be observant about your patterns will create a better path for your relationships in general and guide you well in negotiating this one if and when you decide trust can be restored.

Think about a relationship in which trust was broken in the past. With the benefit of hindsight, what issues or harmful baggage did you contribute to that relationship?

_____

_____

_____

_____

What is a relationship in which you are currently looking for reconciliation—returning to a cordial standing? What are you expecting from the other party in order to experience reconciliation?

_____

_____

_____

_____

In that relationship, is there anything for which you want to apologize for and ask for forgiveness?

_____

_____

_____

_____

GROUP DISCUSSION

Icebreaker

Choose one of the following questions to begin your group's discussion on "Repairing Trust (Part 2)."

- When did something important in your home break—a piece of furniture, a family heirloom, an appliance, and so on? How did you respond?
  or
- When eating at a restaurant for the first time, how do you typically decide what you want to order? What is your process?

Content Review

What ideas or principles did you find most interesting from Chapters 15–16 of *Trust*?

_____

_____

_____

What questions have been on your mind since reading those chapters? Or, what seemed confusing that you'd like to have resolved?

_____

_____

_____

As a reminder, the first step in repairing trust after a betrayal is healing from that betrayal. This is a necessary step. Unfortunately, it often gets missed or overlooked—largely because the pain is coloring our next moves in the aftermath of broken trust.

Sometimes we want to move forward as quickly as possible in hopes that the pain will ebb just as quickly.

The second step is to move beyond anger and turn toward forgiveness. Usually, this turn should occur *after* we've had ample time to heal. Once you are in a stable place, you can take the steps to let go of your anger and extend forgiveness. Best of all, you can make that choice regardless of what the other party says or does. They do not have the power to control what you choose to do.

Now it's time to take a deeper look at the third step for repairing trust, which is to *ponder what you really want.*

I know "ponder" isn't a common word in the world today, but I've chosen it specifically because it communicates the kind of deep thinking and serious consideration that is needed for this step. You have the ability to choose which direction you go after a betrayal. Yes, there will be people pressuring you to move in this direction or that direction—including the person or company who perpetrated the betrayal. You will have lots of opinions thrown your way about how you should respond.

Ultimately, though, the choice is yours. You get to decide where you want to go. In order to make that decision well, it's critical that you examine the primary scenarios in a thorough way. And it is important to have trusted advisers to think through the options with you. What are the consequences if you move in this direction? What are the potential benefits if you move in that direction?

When you put in the work of truly pondering what you want, you place yourself in a much better position to achieve just that.

Do you typically find it easy or difficult to articulate what you want in a given situation? Explain.

_____

_____

_____

_____

What are some ways outside help and opinions can be helpful when determining what you want moving forward?

_____

_____

_____

_____

What are some ways outside help and opinions can be harmful?

_____

_____

_____

_____

The fourth step in the process for repairing trust is to *figure out if reconciliation is available*. As a reminder, being reconciled means returning the relationship to a good standing. It does not mean that everything is fixed and trust can safely be restored. That might be the outcome, but it might not.

Two things are necessary for reconciliation to occur in a relationship where trust was broken. The first is for the offending party to recognize what they did wrong, accept responsibility for their actions, and apologize. The second is for the person who was harmed to offer forgiveness (which is the focus of step 2).

Once those two criteria have been met, the relationship can return to a more neutral place, rather than existing in brokenness. As I wrote on page 199 of the *Trust* trade book:

> All this step involves is "apology accepted" and "relations restored." You're letting the person know that you no longer hold the offense against them and that it no longer comes between the two of you.

You can move toward feeling that the problem is in the past and move forward in whatever relationship you deem appropriate. This is the stance that many ex-spouses take with each other in co-parenting, for example.

This is usually all it takes to reach the point of reconciliation. Remember, *I'm not referring to trusting again. I'm only talking about reconciling the relationship to a good, forgiven place.* You may or may not be able to extend trust again. This depends on many other factors as we shall see. **Reconciliation is only the first step.** But with forgiveness from your side, and clear ownership and responsibility and remorse and repentance on the other side, you can at least return to a place where you are okay with each other.

How can we tell whether a person's apology is sincere? What do you consider to be reliable evidence of sincerity?

_____

_____

_____

_____

When have you been in a relationship that moved from "hurt" to "reconciled"? What allowed you to feel comfortable in that place?

_____

_____

_____

_____

What should we be cautious of or wary about when we consider moving a relationship from "hurt" to "reconciled"?

_____

_____

_____

As you do the work of pondering what you want and determining whether reconciliation is an option, it will be helpful to know who you are dealing with. Meaning, what kind of person (or group of people) will you be engaging with, and what can you expect from them?

Are they wise? Do they have the ability to listen, hear what others are saying, and consider adjusting their course? Can they accept constructive criticism? Do they have a desire for things to be better rather than seeking ways to keep hurting you?

Or, are you dealing with someone who is a fool or a mocker? Do they seem unable to accept responsibility or demonstrate empathy for what you have experienced? Are they more angry than contrite? Do they keep trying to prove that they are right and you are wrong?

Lastly, is it possible you are dealing with evil behavior? Do they seem intent on harming you? Have they plotted revenge against you, or do you strongly sense they are scheming to bring you down in some way?

Obviously, if you are dealing with the third type of person, then reconciliation (and trust) needs to be taken off the table. Have as little to do with such people as possible.

How can the five essentials of trust help us evaluate what kind of person (or people) we are dealing with when it comes to the possibility of reconciliation?

_____

_____

_____

What are some ways we can evaluate our own areas of wisdom and foolishness? How can we get an accurate picture of ourselves?

_____

_____

_____

_____

Case Study

Amika does not know what to do with her mother. Their relationship always felt strained growing up, but her mother had the power. Whenever Amika tried to assert herself or set boundaries, her mother shut things down and demanded that she fall in line. There was not an option for "my way or the highway"; it was only "my way."

Now as an adult, Amika has three children of her own. One of them is out of the house, one is in college, and the third is in high school. Amika's family lives many hours away from her mother, but they stay in touch regularly through phone, text, and social media.

Amika has often felt frustrated by her mother's continued attempts to control her—telling Amika what to do, asking to know personal details, and offering her opinion on seemingly every situation under the sun. Once again, whenever Amika has tried to set healthier boundaries in the past, her mother refuses to comply. She uses guilt and manipulation to keep power in their relationship.

Recently, however, things have gone too far. Amika discovered that her mother has contacted many of Amika's friends through Facebook and even phone conversations. Then, yesterday, Amika's mother disclosed something personal and embarrassing about Amika's life to one of those friends. That friend shared the disclosure with Amika because it made her friend feel uncomfortable.

Amika feels furious that her mother is intruding so deeply into her life as an adult—and doing so behind her back. She is desperate to figure out how to have a healthy relationship with her mother, whom she still loves, or to determine if such a thing is even possible.

What are some specific ways Amika's mother has broken trust with her daughter?

_____

_____

_____

_____

How would you advise Amika to go about "assessing the damage" done by her mother? Meaning, how can she determine any other ways her mother has stuck her nose into her life without telling her?

_____

_____

_____

_____

At some point, Amika will need to ponder what she wants from this relationship with her mother. What are the main scenarios or alternatives she could pursue? What would you say is the best-case scenario? Worst-case? What are the various levels of relationship that are possible with her?

_____

_____

_____

_____

What might it look like for Amika and her mother to reach a point of reconciliation?

_____

_____

_____

_____

Wrap Up

Remember these truths as you conclude this discussion of session 6:

- The third step in repairing trust is for you to ponder what you want moving forward. This includes thinking seriously about the different possibilities for the relationship in question and determining which possibility you want to pursue.
- The fourth step in repairing trust involves assessing whether reconciliation is possible. Reconciliation means returning the relationship to a place of amicability and "good standing." It does not mean trust is restored.
- Part of determining whether reconciliation is possible includes assessing the person (or people) who broke your trust. Are they repentant, willing to take responsibility, and apologetic?

What is one action you would like to take this week based on what you've learned?

_____

_____

_____

_____

Moreover if your brother sins against you, go and tell him his fault between you and him alone. If he hears you, you have gained your brother. But if he will not hear, take with you one or two more, that "by the mouth of two or three witnesses every word may be established." And if he refuses to hear them, tell it to the church. But if he refuses even to hear the church, let him be to you like a heathen and a tax collector.

—Matthew 18:15–17 NKJV

And when you stand praying, if you hold anything against anyone, forgive them, so that your Father in heaven may forgive you your sins.

— Mark 11:25 NIV

REPAIRING TRUST (PART 3)

In this session, you will:

- Explore the fifth step for repairing trust: *assess trustworthiness to determine if trust is an option.*
- Explore the sixth step for repairing trust: *look for evidence of real change.*
- Join with others to review these themes and discuss how they apply to your lives and your community.

> Prior to engaging this session, read chapters 17–19 in the *Trust* trade book.

Personal Study

The bulk of the material in the *Trust* book, along with this study guide, has focused on two sets of information: 1) the five essentials of trust and 2) the six steps for repairing trust. Those two sets are like the outer boundaries of a road leading toward vital, renewed, and healthy experiences with trust.

We've already discussed four steps in the process of repairing trust. Now let's continue with the final two steps, starting with . . .

Step 5: Assess Trustworthiness to Determine If Trust Is an Option

As we saw in the previous session, it's not healthy to jump from trust that is completely broken all the way to trust that is completely restored in a single leap. Repairing trust is a process. One that takes significant time and investment from both parties involved.

That process begins when the injured person is able to heal and then extend forgiveness to the offending party. Once forgiveness has been extended, the injured party can consider allowing the relationship to move toward reconciliation. The relationship is once more affable, and perhaps even friendly. But it is not yet a trust relationship.

As we reach step 5 in this process, it's time for the injured party to determine whether they are willing to continue moving forward toward a renewed, repaired version of trust.

As I wrote on page 211 of the *Trust* book:

> After you've taken the first four steps in the process of repairing trust, it's time to take step 5 and determine whether the option of rebuilding trust with the person who betrayed you is viable. The way to do this is to use the five essentials of trust as a guide. These elements of trust are just as helpful in knowing if you can trust someone *again* as they are in determining whether you can trust someone in the first place.

Review the section called "Drew: The Model of the Model" on pages 211–213 of the book, focusing specifically on Drew and Bella's journey toward restored trust. Reading the material from Bella's perspective, which of those steps would feel most painful to you? Why?

_____

_____

_____

_____

Looking at that story from Drew's perspective, what specific actions did he take that seem most significant for his goal of repairing trust with his wife?

_____

_____

_____

_____

As you saw from Drew and Bella's story, the fifth step for repairing trust intersects with the five essentials of trust. Specifically, the five essentials are the best tool to evaluate whether trust can be—and/or should be—extended once more.

This takes work. Both parties must look honestly at their relationship in the past to understand better what went wrong. Which of the essentials of trust was not met, or was lacking in a way that allowed the violation to occur?

Take a few moments to practice that kind of work using the material below.

Think back to a relationship in which you experienced a betrayal of trust, whether you were the one who broke trust or for whom trust was broken. (It's okay if you use a relationship you already wrote about earlier in this study guide.)

In the space below, use the five essentials of trust to evaluate what went wrong in that relationship.

Understanding: What major needs were not properly understood, communicated, or respected?

_____

_____

_____

_____

Motive: How did selfishness or self-centeredness or one-sidedness cause damage in the relationship?

_____

_____

_____

Ability: What skills, resources, or expanded availability would have been helpful (and potentially transformational) in the relationship?

_____

_____

_____

Character: Which character traits, either missing or needed and not displayed, played a big role in trust being broken?

_____

_____

_____

Track Record: In what ways were troubling signs or past behaviors that pointed to future harm in the relationship not seen or not addressed?

_____

_____

_____

After exploring what previously went wrong in a relationship that resulted in broken trust, it's also critical to look toward the future. What are specific things you need to be changed or addressed in order for a repaired trust to hold firm? What steps will both parties take to seek a better outcome after this potential second chance?

Think of a relationship in which trust is currently strained, or even broken. In the space below, follow the five essentials of trust to outline specific actions you need to take in order for trust to be restored in that relationship.

Understanding: **What is essential to you for the other party to really hear and understand so that you can put your heart, or wallet, in their hands again?**

_____

_____

_____

What specific behaviors will you need to see to begin to feel secure that they are listening and understanding?

_____

_____

_____

Motive: **What specific behaviors will you need to see to demonstrate the other person's motives?**

_____

_____

_____

What specific behaviors will you need to not see?

_____

_____

_____

Ability: What are the biggest personal or professional skills that you will require to make this relationship work?

_____

_____

_____

Where do you need to reassign roles or seek out new abilities to help the relationship flourish?

_____

_____

_____

Character: What personal or moral traits will you need to see from the other person in order to trust again?

_____

_____

_____

How will you respond to failures along the way?

_____

_____

_____

Track Record: How will both parties' actions and attitudes be monitored in the future?

_____

_____

_____

What landmarks will determine whether you are moving in the right direction?

_____

_____

_____

Step 6: Look for Evidence of Real Change

Once you begin the process of moving forward in a repaired-trust relationship, the biggest questions on your mind will likely be: *Is this working? Have they really changed? Can these good feelings continue, or am I going to be hurt again?*

Unfortunately, none of us can predict the future. Trust that was broken before certainly can be broken again, even when one or both parties in the relationship have grown.

We do not know whether or not trust will be broken again. People do change and grow, but sometimes they don't. Relationships do heal, but sometimes they don't.

And, much like a broken bone, fractured trust can oftentimes heal back with more strength and resiliency than was present originally. Or, a person can fail to do the work needed to make it heal.

Since we don't know, it is a bad strategy to wear blinders and just "hope" that everything will be okay.

Your best strategy for moving forward in a repaired-trust relationship is to tread cautiously and look specifically for genuine evidence that the offending party is pursuing the path that shows they are doing what is needed to give you confidence in giving the "second chance." Call it the "trust but verify" approach.

Review the "Eleven Indicators of True Change" on pages 239–250 of the **Trust** *book. In your own words, write a brief explanation of each indicator in the space below.*

Admission of Need:

_____

_____

_____

_____

Verifiable Involvement in a Proven Change Process:

_____

_____

_____

_____

A Structured Approach:

_____

_____

_____

_____

Skilled Help:

_____

_____

_____

_____

New Experiences and Skills:

_____

_____

_____

_____

Self-Sustaining Motivation:

_____

_____

_____

_____

The Presence of Support:

_____

_____

_____

_____

Some Evidence of Change:

_____

_____

_____

_____

Monitoring Systems:

_____

_____

_____

_____

If Applicable, Total Transparency:

_____

_____

_____

_____

Willingness to Be Questioned:

_____

_____

_____

_____

GROUP DISCUSSION

Icebreaker

Choose one of the following questions to begin your group's discussion on "Repairing Trust (Part 3)."

- What's the most complex thing you have personally repaired (or tried to repair)? What did you learn from that process?
  _or_
- When have you observed or experienced trust restored in a meaningful way?

Content Review

What ideas or principles did you find most interesting from chapters 17–19 of _Trust_?

_____

_____

_____

_____

What questions have been on your mind since reading those chapters?
Or, what seemed confusing that you'd like to have resolved?

_____

_____

_____

_____

_____

We are approaching the end of this study guide, and in this session specifically we will discuss the final two steps in the process for repairing trust. So, this is a good time to emphasize once again that repairing trust is not a linear process. It is unlikely you will proceed neatly and logically from step 1 to step 2 to step 3 and all the way through to step 6. There will be overlap. There will be bouncing from step to step, and back again.

In addition, there will be mistakes and misunderstandings. Even failures. Building trust from scratch is often a messy process, and repairing trust is even more so. It's important to determine on the front end how both parties will handle setbacks.

With those caveats established, the fifth step in repairing trust is to *determine whether trust is an option*. This is similar to step 4, in which the wronged party works to determine whether reconciliation is a reasonable option.

Once both parties are able to reconcile—once the relationship is returned to a good and cordial standing—the door is open to continue moving that relationship toward a restored trust if that is what you desire.

How does trust get reestablished after it is broken? The same way it was established in the first place—through the five essentials of trust. (Actually, if trust was offered prematurely before the betrayal, using the five essentials to repair that connect will result in a much stronger, much more genuine trust relationship.)

In what ways does reviewing the five essentials of trust through the lens of repairing a relationship feel different from establishing trust from scratch?

_____

_____

_____

_____

In what ways does it feel similar?

_____

_____

_____

_____

How would you describe step 5 to someone who was unfamiliar with the six steps for repairing trust?

_____

_____

_____

_____

As you work the process of rebuilding trust, it's important to look both backward and forward. Meaning, both parties do well to evaluate their past experiences through the five essentials of trust in order to determine what went wrong. Was trust ever firmly established in the relationship? If so, what factors allowed it to be weakened and broken? What should be different this time?

In addition to exploring the past, it's also necessary to use the five essentials of trust to cast a new vision for the future. A healthier vision. This will require lots of conversation and lots of intentionality. But it will open the door for a deep and sustainable trust.

One more reminder: it's best to work through this step under the guidance and support of outside help. As I wrote on page 229 of the *Trust* book:

> As you do the work of repairing trust, my strong suggestion is to figure out in the very beginning *who will help you in this process?* In order to work on the five elements, most repair journeys that are successful enlist the right help from outside, meaning outside of the relationship. In fact, having some people to help you walk the path is required.
>
> There are a million possibilities for help, and all are valid: counselors, mentors, coaches, therapists, consultants, trainings, developmental performance paths, board interventions, wise people in your church or community, and others.

How do you respond emotionally to the idea of counseling or therapy? Why?

_____

_____

_____

_____

Review "The Five Essentials Road Map for Your Situation" on page 233 of the *Trust* book. Which elements or questions in that road map seem most significant for living out a repaired-trust relationship?

_____

_____

_____

_____

The final step in the process of repairing trust is to *look for evidence of real change*. Once again, people or companies should not move from "untrusted" to "fully trusted" in a single leap. Trust should be restored slowly. Cautiously.

As you move forward in a repaired-trust relationship, do so by extending small amounts of trust in controlled situations. Take baby steps and observe what happens. Are those small extensions of trust rewarded? Does the ground feel stable? Do you feel comfortable to continue offering a little more trust, and then a little more?

In other words, do you see real evidence of real change in the other party? As I wrote in the *Trust* trade book:

> No one can predict the future. There are no guarantees that the other person will always be trustworthy. The only one who can assure trust-worthiness in the future is the one who broke the trust in the past. That's right, the person who broke your trust decides whether or not to earn your trust going forward. Their behavior will make the determination. All you need to do is to observe it, to watch it from the bleachers, so to speak. You do not have to be a fortune teller. You have to be an observer of their behavior.

Read through the "Eleven Indicators of True Change" on pages 239–252 of the *Trust* book. Which of the indicators seem surprising or confusing? Why?

_____

_____

_____

_____

Which of the indicators would feel most significant if you were attempting to repair trust with someone who had betrayed you?

_____

_____

_____

_____

In your opinion, what are some major red flags that would indicate the other party is not truly working the path toward real change?

_____

_____

_____

_____

Case Study

Rodrigo is working through a second chance for Spencer, his business partner, and he knows it will be a work in progress for some time. The two men founded a software company together. Spencer is the programming whiz, while Rodrigo is the one more focused on the business and finances.

At the launch, Spencer took the title of CEO, while Rodrigo was content to be the chief operations officer. Over the course of their first year together, however, it became clear that Spencer associated the role of CEO with "king"—and that he believed bosses can do whatever they want, without regard for what happens when they do.

The company did very well out of the gates. Revenue and capital were not a problem. But Spencer consistently made undisciplined financial choices that worried Rodrigo. (Not to mention created a lot of messes for Rodrigo to clean up.) As they grew a team of employees, Spencer began playing favorites with team members he liked more than others. He gave people the day off on a whim. He promised "unofficial" bonuses. He invited people to hang out in his office for long periods of time.

At that point, the board had seen enough. They brought in a consultant to try and connect with Spencer and show him the potential consequences of his actions on the leadership and financial and cultural aspects of the company. Ultimately, the consultant concluded that Spencer was stuck in his belief that CEO meant "I can do anything." So, the board elevated Rodrigo to CEO and assigned Spencer a subordinate role, with the hope that he would submit and learn from his mistakes.

It's been a few months since that change in positions, and so far, Spencer seems to have received the message. He has curtailed his behavior and seems to be learning from his mistakes. He continues to perform well in his area of expertise, and he has not shown any ill will toward Rodrigo. There is hope that things can settle into a stable working environment and hope that the company still has an exciting future.

In what ways did Spencer violate or ignore the five essentials of trust?

_____

_____

_____

_____

What were the different alternatives Rodrigo and the board likely considered in determining what they wanted to happen moving forward? (What other options did they have?) Why do you think they kept Spencer around?

_____

_____

_____

_____

_____

What are some specific ways that Spencer could demonstrate real change to Rodrigo, the board, and his other team members in the months to come?

_____

_____

_____

_____

_____

In your opinion, how vigilant should Rodrigo be in looking over Spencer's shoulder to make sure he is staying in line?

_____

_____

_____

_____

Wrap Up

Remember these truths as you conclude this discussion of session 7:

- The fifth step in repairing trust is to determine whether trust can be restored or whether it's best to keep the relationship at the "reconciled" stage. The five essentials of trust are the best tool to determine whether you should move forward.
- The sixth step for repairing trust is to look for evidence of real change. As you extend trust bit by bit, be specific in evaluating how the other party handles it.
- As you work through these final steps in the process for repairing trust, it's best to do with the support of someone outside the relationship—a counselor, a consultant, a mentor, a trusted friend, etc.

What is one action you would like to take this week based on what you've learned?

_____

_____

_____

_____

And we are sending along with them our brother whose earnestness has been proven many times and in many ways, and now even more so by his great confidence in you.

— 2 Corinthians 8:22 BSB

AVOIDING THE SAME MISTAKES

In this session, you will:

- Explore the concept of misplaced trust—the mistakes or omissions that put others in a place to betray us or break our trust.
- Explore five common reasons why people choose to trust others when they should not.
- Join with others to review these themes and discuss how they apply to your lives and your community.

Prior to engaging this session, read chapters 20–21 in the *Trust* trade book.

Personal Study

You've reached the final session in this study guide for *Trust*. But I sincerely hope you have not come to the end of your interest and exploration on the subject of trust. As I wrote all the way back in session 1, trust is the fuel for every aspect of our lives. Therefore, growing in your ability to trust well will reap benefits for every aspect of your life.

Our goal in this final session is to zero in on some of the common mistakes or realities that cause people to misplace their trust—to offer trust when they really should not. After all, one of the ways to avoid betrayal is to not extend trust to people or organizations who are likely to break it.

Consider these thoughts from pages 257–258 of the *Trust* book:

> Think for a moment about the immune system in the human body because we can learn some lessons about trust when we consider how it works. It's highly developed and complicated, but in the most basic terms, it protects us and keeps us healthy. When it works properly, it either keeps us from contracting a disease or infection or it fights off germs that have gained access to our bodies. One part of our immunity is innate; it's the equipment that comes from being human—skin, enzymes in tears and secretions, stomach acid, and other mechanisms to fight infection. It treats all germs and foreign substances the same way and acts quickly when they try to enter the body. The other part of our immune system is adaptive or specialized. This is the part that learns to recognize and respond to specific germs and has the ability to remember them and fight them the next time they try to enter the body. . . .
>
> Misplaced trust happens in the heart, mind, and soul like infection happens in the body. We often either don't have adequate "systems" in our hearts, minds, and souls to protect us from untrustworthy people to begin with or our immunities are down in some way, or we didn't learn from past "trust infections" to develop the ability to recognize and fight them off when they return.

Use the space below to make a brief list of connections or relationships in which you misplaced your trust.

_____

_____

_____

_____

With the benefit of hindsight, what would you do differently if you could evaluate the connections or relationships all over again?

_____

_____

_____

_____

One of the benefits of exploring the past is that doing so allows us to learn lessons that apply to the present—and to the future. I have helped many individuals and organizations perform a "trust autopsy" after moments of significant betrayal. Through those encounters, I have noticed several factors that rise to the surface more commonly than others.

Let's briefly explore five reasons why people choose to extend trust when they should not.

First, we misplace our trust when the appropriate equipment for evaluating was never installed in our minds, hearts, and experience. Most people receive at least some training on how to judge the character of others, when and how to set boundaries, and what types of people are trustworthy. More and more, however, I am noticing a large number of individuals who reach adulthood missing one or more of those tools.

Tragically, it's also true that many people are raised in abusive situations. They don't learn how to identify negative character traits and untrustworthy people because they are raised by such people—or they spend a lot of time around such people.

What are some specific ways you were trained in how to evaluate other people for potential trustworthiness?

_____

_____

_____

Based on your life experiences, how would you assess the quality of your "trust equipment"?

1	2	3	4	5	6	7	8	9	10

(Poor)   *(Excellent)*

The second reason people commonly mis-evaluate trust opportunities is because they don't learn from past experiences. When their trust is abused, or when they are harmed by betrayal, they don't learn new principles and adapt their behavior.

Instead, they continue to repeat harmful patterns of trusting the wrong people, getting hurt, working to heal, and then trusting the wrong people again.

Review the bullet list beginning on page 285 of the *Trust* book. That list offers several reasons why people fail to learn and continue repeating harmful patterns. Which items on that list ring true for your experiences?

_____

_____

_____

What are some specific lessons you have learned from your past when it comes to what makes a person worthy of your trust?

_____

_____

_____

The third reason people misplace trust in others is a lack of boundaries. Or, the lack of the skills necessary for setting boundaries. The basic definition of a boundary is a hard line, or limit, that describes where you end and someone else begins. Meaning, we set boundaries when we are able to take a stand and say, "This is not acceptable for me; therefore, I will not allow this to continue."

Setting boundaries is a critical skill for all relationships. As I wrote in the *Trust* book:

> Being able to talk about something that bothers us, quickly, keeps problems from growing larger and prevents us from trusting people who are not trustworthy. Many trust betrayals should have been nipped in the bud, but little things were ignored or enabled because someone was conflict avoidant. They didn't have the boundaries that enabled them to say, "This can't continue." We all need to develop the skills to deal with conflict before it leads to a meltdown.

Think about your current closest relationships. What are some specific boundaries you have set in those relationships? Give examples.

_____

_____

_____

How would you evaluate your ability to set boundaries in personal relationships?

1   2   3   4   5   6   7   8   9   10

(Poor)   *(Excellent)*

What about boundaries in business or professional relationships?

1   2   3   4   5   6   7   8   9   10

(Poor)   *(Excellent)*

Fourth, people often extend trust inappropriately because they were not exposed to the harmful consequences of broken trust in the past. In the same way that children who are exposed to lots of bacteria early on typically develop strong immune systems, people who are "exposed" to many types of relationships quickly learn some basic skills for protecting themselves against schemers and manipulators.

However, sometimes people are simply too naïve or too inexperienced to make those kinds of healthy evaluations. They have never experienced people who betray trust, and they are good trustworthy people. As a result, they can't conceive in their wildest dreams of intentionally harming others or acting solely in their own self-interest; therefore, they also cannot imagine others treating them in those ways.

Basically, they lack the wisdom we typically gain from experience—especially painful experiences.

In your own words, how would you describe the difference between this lack of "trust antibodies" and the lack of "trust equipment" described earlier?

_____

_____

_____

_____

Does this lack of trust antibodies ring true for your life? Why or why not?

_____

_____

_____

_____

Finally, people sometimes fall victim to misplaced trust because they lack a tribe or support system. Being wise yourself is very helpful. Having access to other people who have developed their own wisdom through their own experiences is just as important and helpful. We benefit as individuals when we can access the collective intelligence and perception of a group of people who want the best for our lives.

Also, as I've mentioned many times throughout these pages, doing the work of building trust is hard. It's difficult. This is especially true when that work includes navigating conflict. We are much stronger at those skills when we have the support of friends and family who can come alongside us, instruct us, pick us up when we're down, and help us stay steered in the right direction.

As the Bible says, "Though one may be overpowered by another, two can withstand him. And a threefold cord is not quickly broken" (Ecc. 4:12 NKJV).

Which relationships in your life boost your ability to make good decisions? Use the space below to make a list.

_____

_____

_____

_____

_____

How often do you make use of those relationships when you need to make important decisions—such as choosing to trust someone?

1   2   3   4   5   6   7   8   9   10

(Rarely)   (Regularly)

Looking back at the five factors that cause us to misplace trust, which of those factors seems like a weakness in your life? Why?

_____

_____

_____

_____

GROUP DISCUSSION

Icebreaker

Choose one of the following questions to begin your group's discussion on "Avoiding the Same Mistakes."

- When have you recently scolded yourself by saying, "How could this happen again?"
  or
- What's one of the biggest relationship lessons you've learned through mistakes?

Can you forgive yourself and learn from the past?

_____

_____

_____

_____

Content Review

What ideas or principles did you find most interesting from chapters 20–21 of *Trust*?

_____

_____

_____

_____

What questions have been on your mind since reading those chapters?
Or, what seemed confusing that you'd like to have resolved?

_____

_____

_____

_____

None of us is perfect when it comes to trust. We all make mistakes: trusting the wrong person, trusting for the wrong reasons, failing to see when trust is fraying at the seams, clinging to connections because we are scared of losing the person hurting us, and more. These missteps are part of what it means to be human.

Thankfully, though, mistakes offer us the opportunity to learn. To adapt. To grow. And the more we are able to educate ourselves through past failures, the more we will avoid those same failures in the future. As the old saying goes: "Fool me once, shame on you. Fool me twice, shame on me."

With that in mind, let's review some of the primary reasons why people make mistakes when it comes to trusting others:

1. Their "trust equipment" was never installed.
2. They fail to learn from experience.
3. They lack boundaries or boundary-setting skills.
4. They never developed "trust antibodies."
5. They don't have a tribe or support system.

What are some of the ways our culture tries to instill "trust equipment" in people? (What does culture tell us about which people should be trusted and which should not?)

_____

_____

_____

_____

_____

How would you describe the concept of boundaries in your own words?
What are they, and why are they important?

_____

_____

_____

_____

What are some of the biggest ways your past experiences have influenced
your present ability to trust?

_____

_____

_____

_____

Where can people find a support system or wise counsel in today's world?

_____

_____

_____

_____

Psalm 101 (NKJV) offers an interesting look into several types of people who should not be trusted:

I will sing of mercy and justice;

To You, O Lord, I will sing praises.

I will behave wisely in a perfect way.

Oh, when will You come to me?

I will walk within my house with a perfect heart.

I will set nothing wicked before my eyes;

I hate the work of those who fall away;

It shall not cling to me.

A perverse heart shall depart from me;

I will not know wickedness.

Whoever secretly slanders his neighbor,

Him I will destroy;

The one who has a haughty look and a proud heart,

Him I will not endure.

My eyes shall be on the faithful of the land,

That they may dwell with me;

He who walks in a perfect way,

He shall serve me.

He who works deceit shall not dwell within my house;

He who tells lies shall not continue in my presence.

Early I will destroy all the wicked of the land,

That I may cut off all the evildoers from the city of the Lord.

What type of people did David determine not to trust?

_____

_____

_____

_____

Where do you see connections between this psalm and what we've explored
throughout this study guide?

_____

_____

_____

_____

Review the additional explanations for misplaced trust in the appendix. Which
ones strike you as most relevant in our culture? Why?

_____

_____

_____

_____

Case Study

Janice feels like she's at rock bottom. Yesterday, she walked out of her lawyer's office
after settling the terms and signing the paperwork for her third divorce in ten years.
She used the same lawyer for all three divorces. She even made a joke about it: "Do
you have one of those punch cards? Like, five separations and the sixth is free?"

But neither she nor her lawyer could laugh.

Janice knows her problem: she keeps getting interested in the same type of man. Handsome and complicated. Strong and mysterious. Totally self-confident and completely convincing. Every time, Janice jumps in with both feet almost from the beginning of the relationship. Every time, the guy gets everything he wants and then decides to hit the road.

Janice keeps telling herself, "I have to change this. I need to do something different." But at the end of the day, she doesn't know how.

She feels completely stuck in a pattern that she never sees until it's too late.

What are some specific questions Janice needs to contemplate in order to help break free from that pattern?

_____

_____

_____

_____

_____

What are some specific actions Janice should take to avoid making the same mistakes again?

_____

_____

_____

_____

_____

Which of the five essentials of trust seems to connect most strongly with Janice's story? Why?

_____

_____

_____

_____

Wrap Up

Remember these truths as you conclude this discussion of session 8:

- We all make mistakes when it comes to trust. The good news is that we can learn from them.
- Often our misplaced trust is the result of equipment or experiences we did not develop during our developmental years.
- The five essentials of trust are a critical tool for improving every aspect of your life.

What is one action you would like to take this week based on what you've learned?

_____

_____

_____

_____

_____

ABOUT THE AUTHOR

DR. HENRY CLOUD is an acclaimed leadership expert, clinical psychologist, and *New York Times* best-selling author. His forty-five books, including the iconic *Boundaries*, have sold nearly twenty million copies worldwide. He has an extensive executive coaching background and experience as a leadership consultant, devoting the majority of his time to working with CEOs, leadership teams, and executives to improve performance, leadership skills, and culture.